# Jonah and the Whale

Written by Sasha Morton
Illustrated by Cherie Zamazing

Ticktock

Long ago, God asked a young man named Jonah to deliver a message. Jonah was to tell the people who lived in a place called Nineveh to stop being unkind to each other. If they didn't change their wicked ways, God would destroy their city!

Unfortunately, Jonah thought everyone should be punished for their bad behaviour, so instead of delivering the message…

…Jonah ran away.

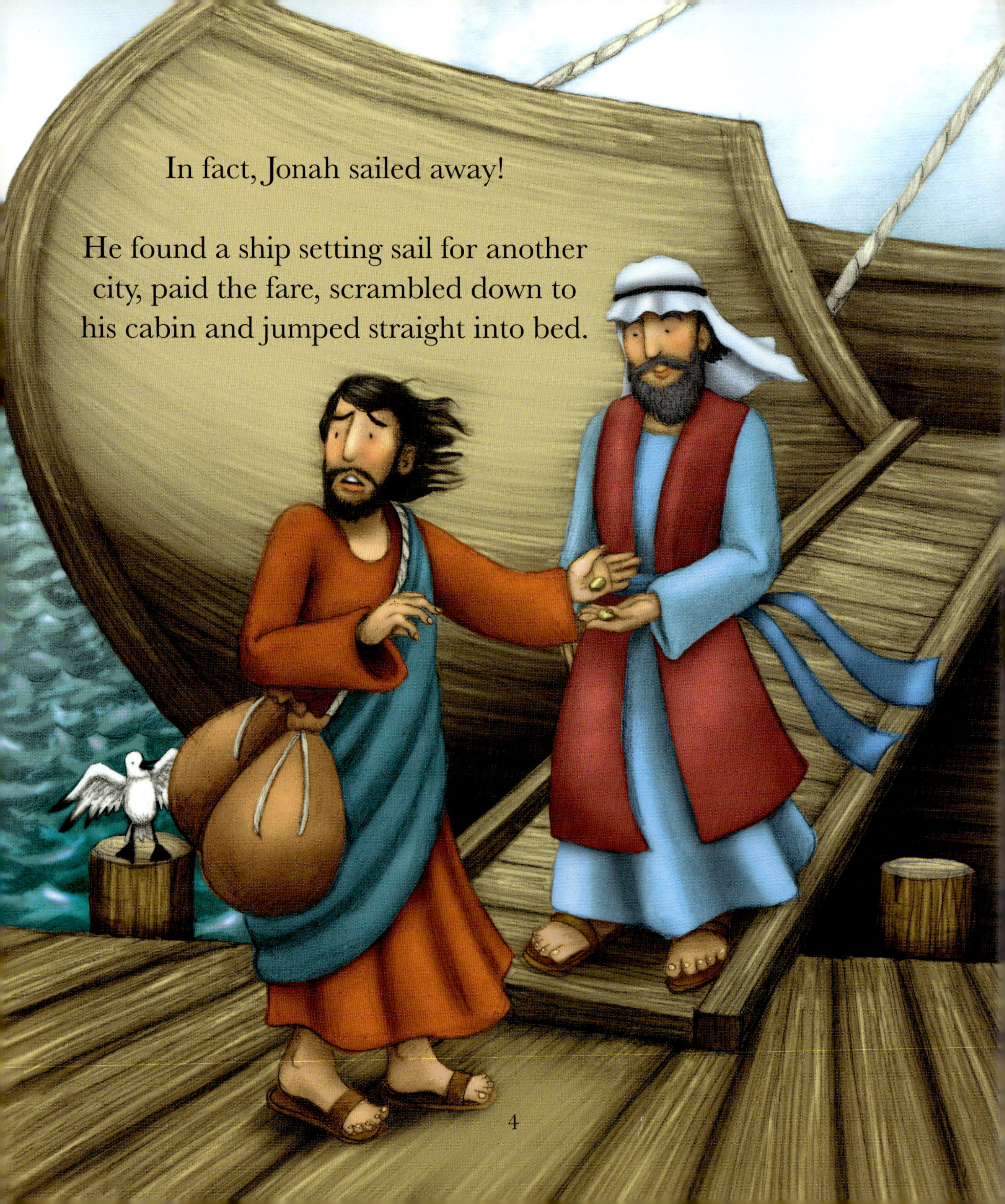

In fact, Jonah sailed away!

He found a ship setting sail for another city, paid the fare, scrambled down to his cabin and jumped straight into bed.

Jonah was so relieved to have avoided carrying out God's plan that he soon fell sound sleep.

But while Jonah snored, a terrible storm began…

Ferocious winds ripped the ship's sails from its mast. Waves taller than buildings crashed over the deck.

The crew threw the cargo overboard to stop the ship from sinking, but the angry sea continued to rush in.

"We must find out which person has sinned, Captain!" shouted one of the superstitious sailors. "He's brought us bad luck."

The captain asked the other sailors but it was none of them. Then he woke Jonah, yelling, "If you have done wrong, please ask your God to forgive you before we all drown!"

At once, Jonah realised that the captain was right. God was punishing him.

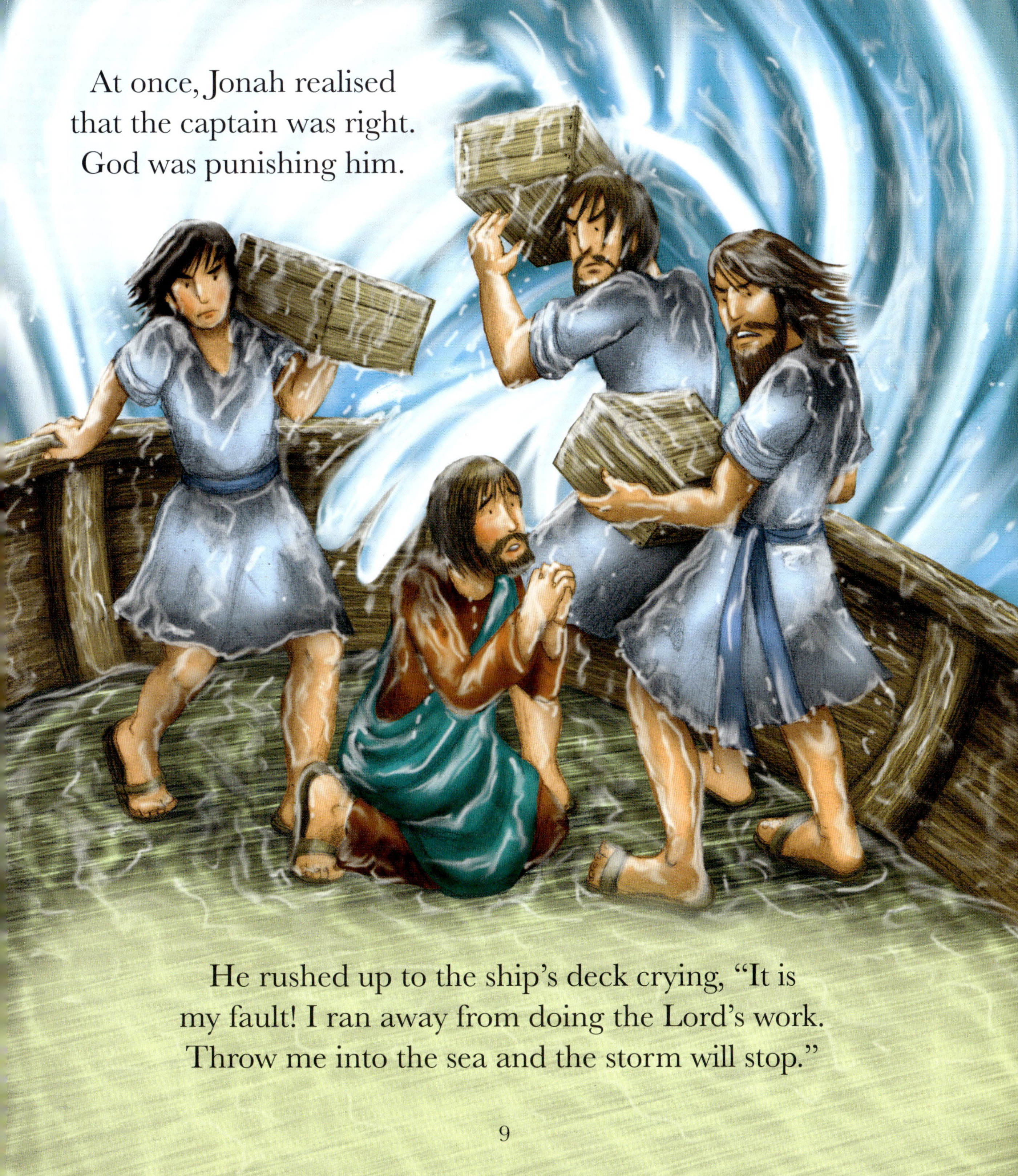

He rushed up to the ship's deck crying, "It is my fault! I ran away from doing the Lord's work. Throw me into the sea and the storm will stop."

Despite trying their hardest to row to safety, eventually the sailors decided they had no choice and they dropped Jonah overboard.

Within moments, a ray of sunlight pierced the black clouds. The foaming sea grew peaceful and the wind lowered to a whisper.

As the skies cleared, the sailors decided
that Jonah's God must have calmed the storm.
They even began to pray to him themselves!

Out at sea, Jonah struggled to the surface, gasping for air.

"Look! He's alive!" shouted the amazed crew.

Then, something really incredible happened…

A huge whale rose up from the depths of the water. It opened its enormous jaws and scooped Jonah into its gaping mouth. In one gulp, Jonah was gone!

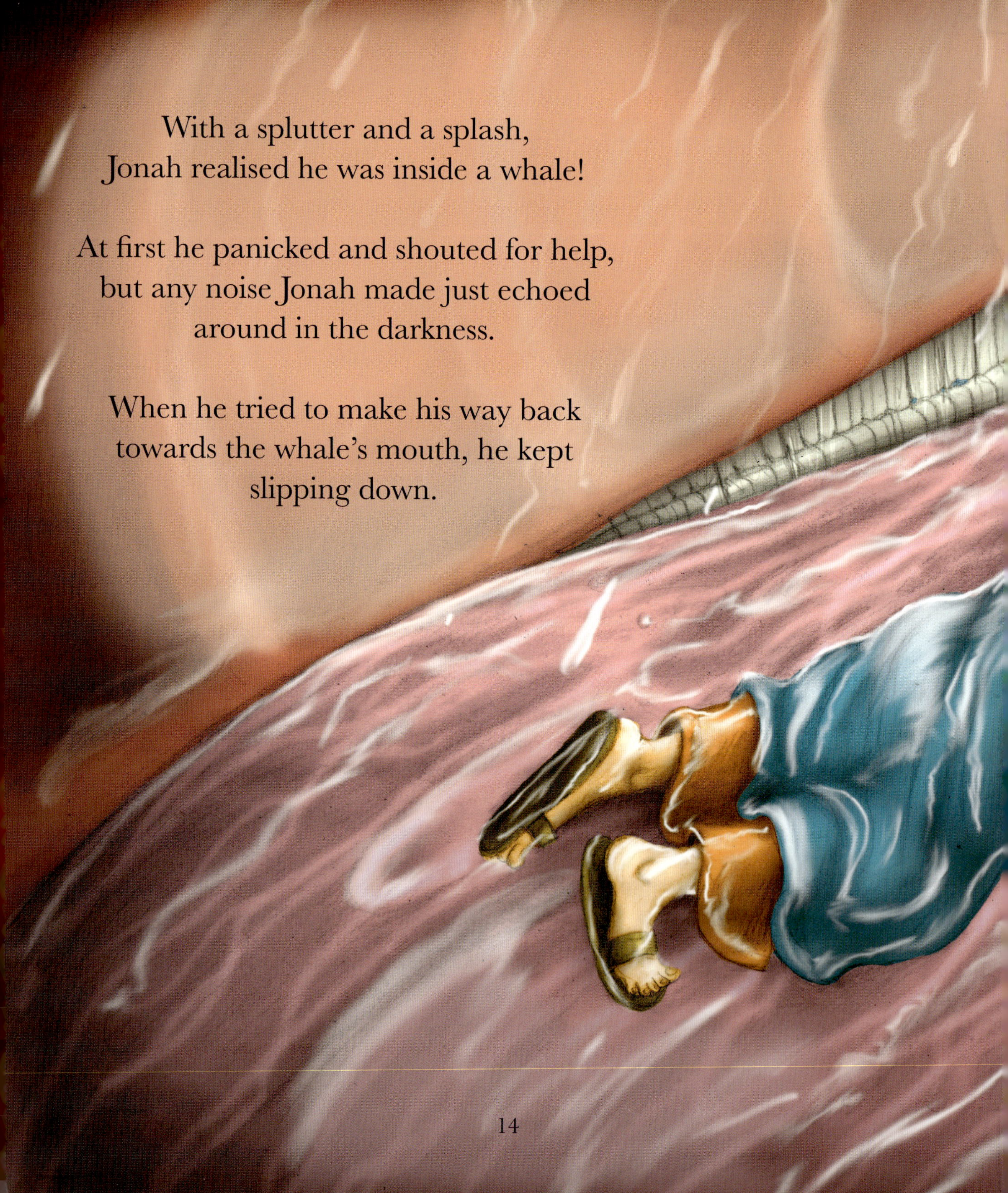

With a splutter and a splash,
Jonah realised he was inside a whale!

At first he panicked and shouted for help, but any noise Jonah made just echoed around in the darkness.

When he tried to make his way back towards the whale's mouth, he kept slipping down.

It was hopeless.
There was no escape.

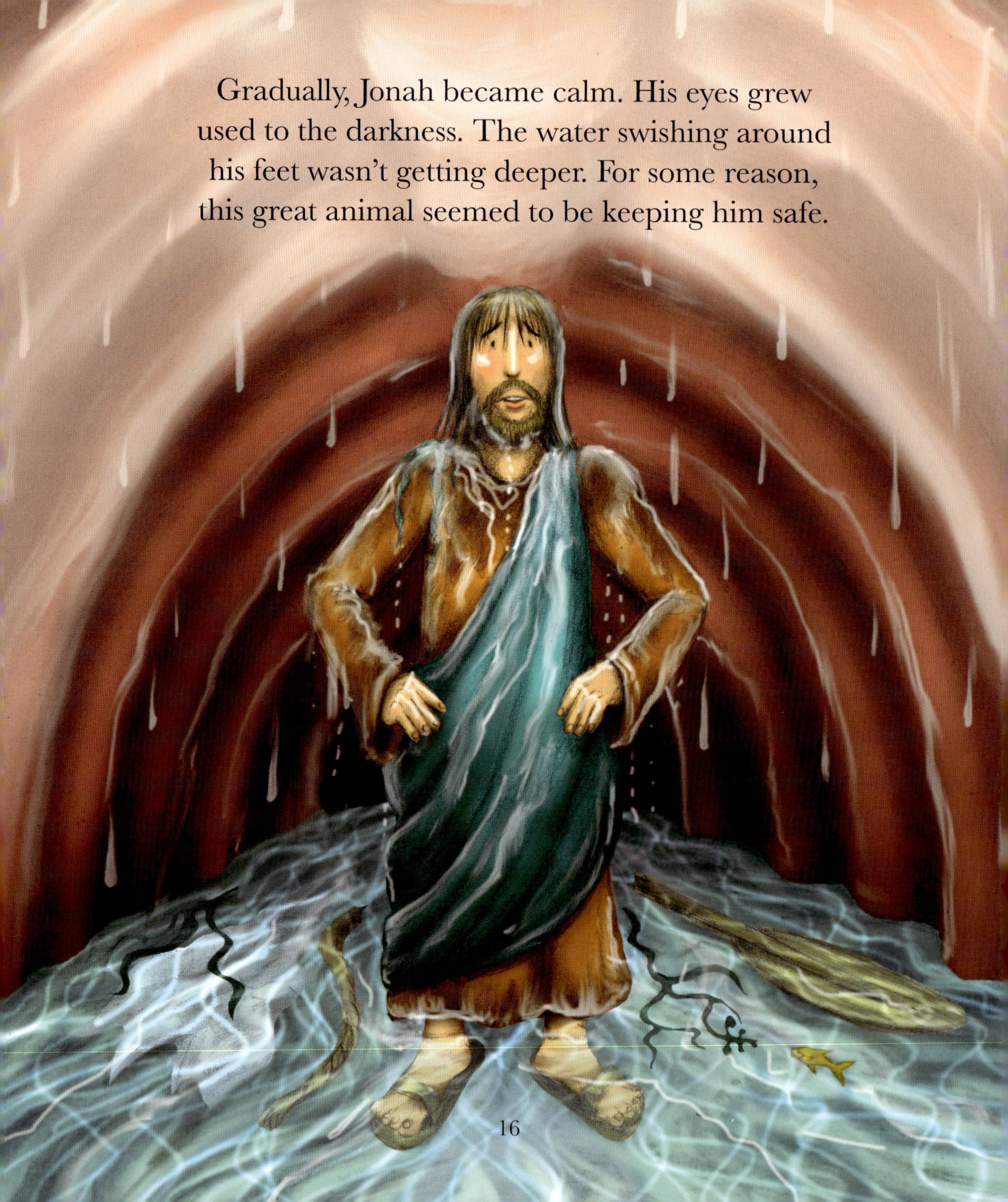

Gradually, Jonah became calm. His eyes grew used to the darkness. The water swishing around his feet wasn't getting deeper. For some reason, this great animal seemed to be keeping him safe.

Jonah decided that God had sent the whale to save him. Immediately, he dropped to his knees and thanked the Lord. As he prayed, Jonah even asked for another chance to do the job he had been given.

Before long, Jonah trusted that God would return him to dry land. For three days and three nights, he waited patiently and prayed.

Finally, something happened…

The great fish stopped moving. Then there was a sudden rush of air and Jonah was thrown forward on a wave of salty water.

He landed face down on a sandy beach in broad daylight, safe at last!

And this time, Jonah did just as God had asked…

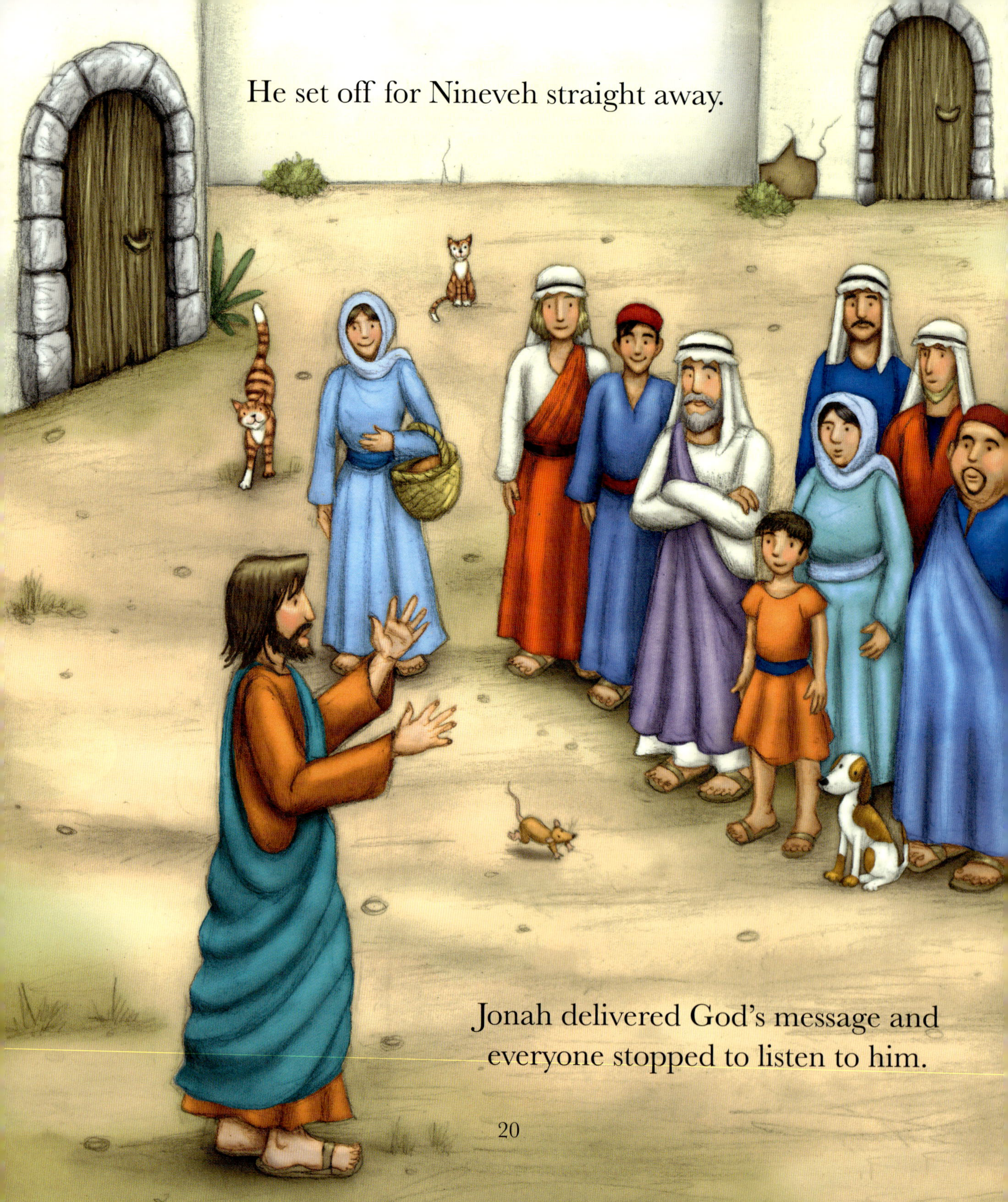

He set off for Nineveh straight away.

Jonah delivered God's message and everyone stopped to listen to him.

"People of Nineveh, you must become better people. If you continue to treat each other badly, the Lord God will destroy your city. But if you pray together and let the Lord love you, you will be saved."

To Jonah's surprise and relief, the people understood his message. He explained how God had saved and forgiven him, and soon, even the King of Nineveh had heard the amazing tale of Jonah and the whale.

Before long, everyone had changed their ways and treated each other with love and respect. They lived peaceful lives and Jonah spent the rest of his days on dry land!

An Hachette UK Company
www.hachette.co.uk

First published in Great Britain in 2014 by Ticktock,
an imprint of Octopus Publishing Group Ltd
Endeavour House
189 Shaftesbury Avenue
London
WC2H 8JY
www.octopusbooks.co.uk
www.ticktockbooks.co.uk



ISBN 978 1 84898 932 0

A CIP record for this book is available from the British Library.

Printed and bound in China

10 9 8 7 6 5 4 3 2 1

With thanks to Jana Burson

Series Editor: Lucy Cuthew Design: Advocate Art
Publisher: Tim Cook Managing Editor: Karen Rigden
Assistant Production Manager: Lucy Carter